CW01022542

Wrap Cookbook

Discover the Many Ways to Enjoy Wraps with Delicious
Wrap Recipes

By
BookSumo Press
All rights reserved

Published by
http://www.booksumo.com

LEGAL NOTES

All Rights Reserved. No Part Of This Book May Be Reproduced Or Transmitted In Any Form Or By Any Means. Photocopying, Posting Online, And / Or Digital Copying Is Strictly Prohibited Unless Written Permission Is Granted By The Book's Publishing Company. Limited Use Of The Book's Text Is Permitted For Use In Reviews Written For The Public.

Table of Contents

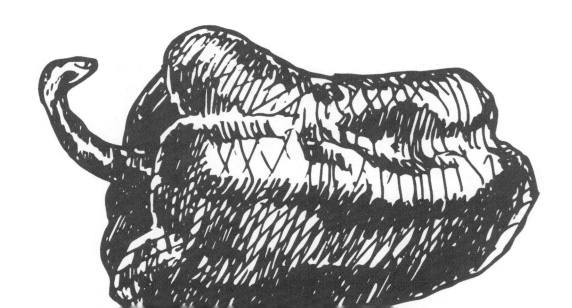

Twin City
Tuna Wraps

Prep Time: 12 mins
Total Time: 12 mins

Servings per Recipe: 2
Calories	203.3
Fat	10.0g
Cholesterol	43.5mg
Sodium	889.6mg
Carbohydrates	6.7g
Protein	20.6g

Ingredients

1 (6 oz.) cans solid white tuna packed in water, drained
1 stalk celery, minced
1 tbsp dill relish
3 tbsp light mayonnaise
2 tbsp red onions, chopped

2 tsp lemon juice, squeezed
1/2 tsp dried dill
1/4 tsp salt
1/4 tsp black pepper
2 fat-free whole wheat tortillas

Directions

1. Get a mixing bowl: Stir in it the tuna, celery, dill relish, mayonnaise, onion, lemon juice, dill, salt, and pepper.
2. Put on the lid and place it in the fridge. Let it sit for an overnight.
3. Spoon the salad mixture into the tortillas. Wrap them burrito style then serve them.
4. Enjoy.

SOUTHWEST
Wraps

Prep Time: 5 mins
Total Time: 5 mins

Servings per Recipe: 4

Calories	208.9
Fat	2.8g
Cholesterol	0.0mg
Sodium	266.8mg
Carbohydrates	36.9g
Protein	9.7g

Ingredients

1 (15 oz.) cans black beans, rinsed and drained
2 tbsp lime juice
2 tbsp orange juice
2 cloves garlic, chopped
1/8 tsp salt
cayenne pepper

3 scallions, chopped
1/4 C. red bell peppers, chopped
4 flour tortillas
salsa

Directions

1. Get a blender: Combine in it the beans, lime juice, orange juice, garlic, salt, and cayenne pepper. Blend them smooth.

2. Pour the mixture into a mixing bowl. Fold into it the bell peppers with scallions.

3. Divide the mixture between the tortillas and spread them in an even layer. Wrap your tortillas tight then serve them.

4. Enjoy.

Bacon
Breakfast Wraps

Prep Time: 30 mins
Total Time: 30 mins

Servings per Recipe: 6
Calories   362.9
Fat   34.2g
Cholesterol   51.4mg
Sodium   649.1mg
Carbohydrates   3.7g
Protein   9.9g

Ingredients

1 lb. turkey bacon, fried, torn into pieces
1 head lettuce, shredded
2 - 3 tomatoes, chopped
Mayonnaise

salt
pepper
flour tortilla

Directions

1. Get a mixing bowl: Toss in it the bacon with lettuce, tomato, mayo, a pinch of salt and pepper.
2. Spoon the mixture 6 to 7 soft tortillas. Wrap it them burrito style.
3. Serve your wraps right away with your favorite toppings.
4. Enjoy.

MANHATTAN
Gourmet Turkey Club Wraps

Prep Time: 25 mins
Total Time: 25 mins

Servings per Recipe: 4
Calories   429.3
Fat   21.1g
Cholesterol   69.9mg
Sodium   1949.6mg
Carbohydrates   26.1g
Protein   34.1g

Ingredients
1/2 C. mustard-mayonnaise blend
4 flour tortillas
1/2 lb. sliced smoked turkey
1/2 lb. sliced honey-roasted ham or roast beef
1 C. shredded smoked provolone cheese
2 C. shredded leaf lettuce
2 medium tomatoes, seeded and chopped

1/2 small purple onion, chopped
8 slices turkey bacon, slices cooked and crumbled
1/2 tsp salt
1/2 tsp pepper

Directions
1. Coat one side of each tortilla with the mayo and mustard mixture.
2. Place the tortillas on serving plates. Arrange over them the turkey followed by ham, cheese, lettuce, tomato, onion, and bacon.
3. Season them with a pinch of salt and pepper.
4. Wrap your tortillas and slice them in half. Serve your wraps right away.
5. Enjoy.

Sonoma
BLT Wraps
(Bacon Lettuce and Tomato)

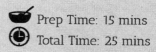 Prep Time: 15 mins

Total Time: 25 mins

Servings per Recipe: 2	
Calories	74.9
Fat	5.0g
Cholesterol	13.5mg
Sodium	290.1mg
Carbohydrates	3.1g
Protein	4.5g

Ingredients

2 slices cooked turkey bacon
1 medium tomatoes, sliced
1 green onion, sliced
1 tbsp shredded cheddar cheese
1 tsp sour cream
nice crispy lettuce

1 dash salt
1 dash pepper
avocado, sliced
1 dash Tabasco sauce

Directions

1. Place a pan over medium heat. Cook in it the bacon until it becomes crisp. Drain it.
2. Heat the tortillas in a pan for 10 to 15 sec on each side. Place them on serving plates.
3. Coat the upper side of the tortillas with sour cream, top it with cheese, lettuce, tomato, bacon, green onion, and avocado.
4. Season them with a pinch of salt and pepper. Wrap your tortillas carefully and slice them in half.
5. Serve your wraps with extra toppings of your choice.
6. Enjoy.

SKYTOP
PB Wraps

🥣 Prep Time: 10 mins
🕐 Total Time: 15 mins

Servings per Recipe: 4
Calories   332.7
Fat   16.5g
Cholesterol   0.0mg
Sodium   412.4mg
Carbohydrates   37.7g
Protein   10.6g

Ingredients
4 (7 - 8 inch) flour tortillas
1/3 C. peanut butter
1 C. chopped granny smith apple
1/4 C. oats & honey granola cereal

Directions
1. Place the tortillas on a cutting board. Coat one side of them with peanut butter.
2. Microwave each tortilla for 10 sec. Transfer to a serving plate.
3. Top them with chopped apple and cereal. Roll them rightly.
4. Serve your wraps right away with extra toppings of your choice.
5. Enjoy.

Summer
Breakfast Wraps

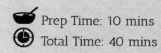 Prep Time: 10 mins

Total Time: 40 mins

Servings per Recipe: 4

Calories	305.4
Fat	18.2g
Cholesterol	376.2mg
Sodium	207.8mg
Carbohydrates	17.7g
Protein	22.3g

Ingredients

8 eggs
1/2 C. milk
1 tbsp sage, chopped
1 tsp thyme, chopped
2 garlic cloves, chopped

1/4 C. pecorino cheese, grated
24 stalks asparagus
2 tbsp extra virgin olive oil

Directions

1. Get a mixing bowl: Whisk in the milk, sage, thyme, garlic, pecorino, a pinch of salt and pepper.
2. Place a saucepan over medium heat. Place in it the asparagus and cover them with hot water.
3. Cook them for 3 min until they become tender. Drain them.
4. Place a large skillet over medium heat. Heat in the olive oil.
5. Pour in it 1/4 of the eggs mix and swirl the pan to spread it in an even layer.
6. Cook the omelet for 1 min on each side until it is done.
7. Place it aside and repeat the process with the remaining eggs mixture.
8. Place 1/4 of the asparagus on an omelet then roll it.
9. Repeat the process with the rest of the omelets and asparagus.
10. Serve them with toppings of your choice.
11. Enjoy.

EASY
Souvlaki Wrap with White Sauce

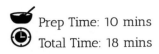

Prep Time: 10 mins
Total Time: 18 mins

Servings per Recipe: 1
Calories	530.0
Fat	22.4g
Cholesterol	104.4mg
Sodium	972.9mg
Carbohydrates	44.3g
Protein	38.9g

Ingredients
Chicken
3 tbsp lemon juice
1/2 tsp dried oregano
2 tsp olive oil
3 garlic cloves, minced
1 boneless skinless chicken breast
Sauce
1/4 C. cucumber, shredded
1/4 C. plain low-fat yogurt

1/2 tbsp lemon juice
1 garlic clove, minced
1/2 small onion, minced
Wrap
1 whole wheat tortilla
tomatoes, slices
2 lettuce leaves
2 tbsp feta cheese

Directions
1. To prepare the chicken:
2. Get a zip lock bag, place in it all the ingredients. Place it in the fridge for 40 min.
3. Get a small mixing bowl: Stir in it all the tzatziki sauce ingredients. Place it in the fridge until ready to serve.
4. Before you do anything else, preheat the grill and grease it. Cook in it the chicken for 4 to 6 min on each side.
5. Slice it and arrange it over the tortilla. Top it with tomato, lettuce, tzatziki sauce and feta cheese.
6. Fold the tortilla burrito style then serve it with extra toppings of your choice.
7. Enjoy.

Memphis Breakfast Wraps

Prep Time: 10 mins
Total Time: 25 mins

Servings per Recipe: 4
Calories   320.2
Fat   25.0g
Cholesterol   158.2mg
Sodium   562.8mg
Carbohydrates   5.3g
Protein   18.2g

Ingredients

1/4 C. A.1. Original Sauce, divided
1 tbsp extra virgin olive oil
1/2 tsp granulated garlic
1/2 tsp thyme leaves
8 oz. sirloin steaks
2 eggs, cracked and whisked
2 pinches sea salt

1/2 tsp red pepper flakes
1 tbsp butter
4 low-carb garden veggie wraps
1/4 C. mayonnaise
1/2 C. fresh spinach leaves
4 cherry tomatoes, sliced
2 oz. goat cheese

Directions

1. Get a mixing bowl: Stir in it half of the original sauce with thyme, garlic and olive oil.
2. Coat the steaks with the mixture.
3. Place a large pan over high heat. Heat in tit the olive oil.
4. Cook in it the steaks for 4 to 5 min on each side. Place them aside to rest for 6 min.
5. Get a mixing bowl: Beat in it the eggs with a salt and pepper flakes.
6. Place a pan over medium heat. Grease it with a cooking spray.
7. Pour in it the egg mixture and cook them scrambled for 1 min.
8. Get a mixing bowl: Whisk in it half of the remaining original sauce with mayo.
9. Lay the wraps on a serving plate. Spread on each one of them 1/3 of the mayo mixture.
10. Arrange over it the spinach leaves, scrambled eggs, tomatoes, and goat cheese.
11. Cut the steaks into strips then place them on top. Roll them burrito style.
12. Serve wraps immediately or wrap them in a piece of foil and place them in the fridge.
13. Enjoy.

NEW HAMPSHIRE
Crab Salad Wraps

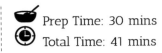

Prep Time: 30 mins

Total Time: 41 mins

Servings per Recipe: 5
Calories	653.9
Fat	36.2g
Cholesterol	296.9mg
Sodium	1517.6mg
Carbohydrates	60.0g
Protein	22.5g

Ingredients
1 (16 oz.) packages imitation crabmeat
2 stalks celery, diced
1 tbsp minced onion
4 oz. cream cheese, softened
1 C. sour cream
1/2 C. mayonnaise
2 tbsp lemon juice
2 tbsp sugar
6 hard-boiled eggs, chopped

1/2 head lettuce
10 flour tortillas

Directions
1. Get a mixing bowl: Shred in it the crab meat. Add to it the celery with onion.
2. Get a mixing bowl: Beat in it the cream cheese, sour cream, mayo, lemon juice and sugar until they become smooth.
3. Add them to the crab mixture and combine them well.
4. Place a tortilla in a serving plate. Top with a thin layer of the crab mixture followed by eggs and lettuce.
5. Fold it and place it aside. Repeat the process with the remaining ingredients.
6. Serve your crab rolls right away.
7. Enjoy.

Queens
Wraps

Prep Time: 10 mins
Total Time: 20 mins

Servings per Recipe: 2
Calories   382.7
Fat   16.3g
Cholesterol   372.0mg
Sodium   656.3mg
Carbohydrates   39.6g
Protein   19.2g

Ingredients

low-fat cooking spray
1/2 red onion, diced
1 small zucchini, grated
8 cherry tomatoes, seeded and quartered
1/4 C. black olives chopped
1/2 C. reduced-fat feta cheese

4 eggs
1 1/2-2 tsp Greek Seasoning, or Italian Seasoning
4 -6 flour tortillas

Directions

1. Get a mixing bowl; Whisk in it the eggs with a pinch of salt and pepper.
2. Place a large pan over medium heat. Coat it with a cooking spray.
3. Sauté in it the onion for 3 min. Stir in the olives with zucchini and tomatoes. Cook them for 1 min.
4. Stir in the eggs and cook them for 4 min. Spoon the mixture into the tortillas. Top them with cheese
5. Roll your tortillas then serve them with extra toppings.
6. Enjoy.

BEEFY
Slaw Wraps

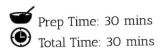

Prep Time: 30 mins
Total Time: 30 mins

Servings per Recipe: 4
Calories	304.0
Fat	17.5g
Cholesterol	77.1mg
Sodium	1102.2mg
Carbohydrates	11.7g
Protein	25.3g

Ingredients

1 head iceberg lettuce, leaves removed
1 lb. ground beef
1/4 C. soy sauce
3 tsp Splenda granular
2 garlic cloves, minced
1 medium onion, diced

1 tbsp red pepper flakes
1 tbsp ginger, grated
2 C. cabbage, chopped

Directions

1. Place a pan over medium heat. Cook in it the onion with beef for 5 min.
2. Stir in the soy, sweetener, garlic, red pepper, ginger, a pinch of salt and pepper.
3. Cook them for 3 min. Stir in the cabbage and cook them for 4 min.
4. Spoon the mixture lettuce leaves. Serve them right away.
5. Enjoy.

Whole Wheat
Apple Wraps

Prep Time: 25 mins
Total Time: 42 mins

Servings per Recipe: 2
Calories   768.0
Fat   17.1g
Cholesterol   31.4mg
Sodium   736.7mg
Carbohydrates   143.3g
Protein   16.1g

Ingredients

2 C. peeled cored and diced tart green apples
1/4 C. raisins
1/4 C. honey
1 tsp ground cinnamon
1/8 tsp salt
1 tbsp butter

1 1/3 C. whole milk
1 C. rolled oats
1 tsp vanilla extract
1/4 C. apple butter
2 10 inch whole wheat tortillas

Directions

1. Get a mixing bowl: Combine in it the apples with raisins, honey, cinnamon, and salt.
2. Place a pan over medium heat. Heat in it the butter.
3. Stir in it the honey apple mixture and let them cook for 9 min.
4. Stir in the milk with oatmeal. Let them cook for an extra 6 min over low heat.
5. Turn off the heat and stir in the vanilla extract.
6. Place the tortillas on a cutting board. Spread the apple mixture over them then roll them.
7. Slice your wraps in half then serve them.
8. Enjoy.

PRE-K
Wraps

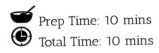 Prep Time: 10 mins

Total Time: 10 mins

Servings per Recipe: 4
Calories   52.5
Fat   0.1g
Cholesterol   0.0mg
Sodium   0.5mg
Carbohydrates   13.4g
Protein   0.6g

Ingredients
4 8-inch fat-free flour tortillas
1/2 C. reduced-fat peanut butter
1/4 C. strawberry all-fruit spread
2 medium bananas, sliced
1/4 C. low-fat granola

Directions
1. Place the tortillas on a cutting board. Spread over them the peanut butter.
2. Arrange over them the bananas followed by granola then roll them. Serve them with some milk.
3. Enjoy.

Ketogenic
Turkey Lunch Box

🍳 Prep Time: 2 mins
🕐 Total Time: 2 mins

Servings per Recipe: 1
Calories   14.2
Fat   0.5g
Cholesterol   0.3mg
Sodium   26.1mg
Carbohydrates   2.2g
Protein   0.4g

Ingredients

1 leaf green lettuce
2 slices of oven roasted turkey breast
2 slices tomatoes
1/2 tsp diced red onion

1/4 tsp mustard
1/4 tsp mayonnaise
salt and pepper

Directions

1. Place a lettuce leaf on a plate. Top it with turkey, onions, mayo, mustard, tomato, a pinch of salt and pepper.
2. Roll lettuce over the filling then serve it.
3. Enjoy.

WACO
Ranch Wraps

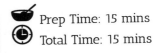

Prep Time: 15 mins

Total Time: 15 mins

Servings per Recipe: 4

Calories	1106.8
Fat	90.5g
Cholesterol	170.4mg
Sodium	1674.7mg
Carbohydrates	36.5g
Protein	39.6g

Ingredients
1 C. ranch dressing
4 flour tortillas, warmed
10 oz. cheese slices, your preference
2 tomatoes, sliced
1 (8 oz.) cream cheese, softened
10 oz. turkey breast, slices

2 avocados, sliced
alfalfa sprout

Directions
1. Get a mixing bowl: Beat in it the cream cheese with ranch dressing until they become creamy.
2. Spoon the mixture into the tortillas and spread them into an even layer.
3. Top them with turkey, cheese, avocados, tomatoes, and sprouts. Roll the tortillas tightly then serve them.
4. Enjoy.

Fathia's
Favorite Wrap

Prep Time: 5 mins
Total Time: 5 mins

Servings per Recipe: 1
Calories	499.3
Fat	18.4g
Cholesterol	0.0mg
Sodium	1015.0mg
Carbohydrates	68.3g
Protein	17.7g

Ingredients

1 (12 inches) tortillas
1/2 C. hummus
1/8 C. cucumber
1/8 C. diced tomato
1/8 C. bell pepper

1/8 C. shoestring carrots
3 slices red onions
alfalfa sprout
lettuce

Directions

1. Warm up the tortillas in the microwave for few seconds.
2. Place them on serving plates. Top them with hummus, veggies, alfalfa sprout, lettuce, a pinch of salt and pepper.
3. Roll your tortillas tight then serve them.
4. Enjoy.

AMISH
Beef Dip for Wraps

🥣 Prep Time: 20 mins
🕐 Total Time: 20 mins

Servings per Recipe: 20
Calories   218.6
Fat   14.2g
Cholesterol   36.4mg
Sodium   780.8mg
Carbohydrates   16.2g
Protein   6.7g

Ingredients
16 oz. cream cheese, softened
12 oz. deli roast beef, chopped
16 oz. baby dill pickles, drained, diced
16 oz. Ritz crackers

Directions
1. Get a mixing bowl: mix in it the cream cheese, chopped beef, and diced pickles.
2. Serve it with crackers right away or place it in the fridge until ready to serve.
3. Enjoy.

Dinner
Wraps
(Ginger Chicken)

Prep Time: 20 mins
Total Time: 20 mins

Servings per Recipe: 8	
Calories	172.6
Fat	6.9g
Cholesterol	54.4mg
Sodium	278.3mg
Carbohydrates	6.9g
Protein	20.7g

Ingredients

1 tsp olive oil
6 (4 oz.) boneless skinless chicken breast halves
1 C. chopped seeded peeled cucumber
3/4 C. chopped red bell pepper
1 1/2 tbsp sugar
1 tbsp minced peeled ginger
3 tbsp lime juice
1 tbsp low sodium soy sauce

1/4 tsp salt
1/4 tsp ground red pepper
1 garlic clove, crushed
1/4 C. creamy peanut butter
2 tbsp water
3 tbsp chopped cilantro
8 (8 inches) fat-free tortillas
4 C. chopped romaine lettuce

Directions

1. Place a large pan over medium heat. Heat in it the oil. Cook in it the chicken for 4 to 6 min on each side.
2. Drain them and shred them.
3. Get a large mixing bowl: Toss in it the chicken with cucumber and bell pepper.
4. Get a food processor: Combine in it the sugar with ginger, lime juice, soy sauce, salt, garlic, and pepper. Blend them smooth.
5. Mix in the water with peanut butter to make the sauce. Add it to the chicken mixture with cilantro and toss them to coat.
6. Heat the tortillas in a microwave. Place them on a cutting board. Spoon the chicken mixture into them.
7. Fold your tortillas tightly then serve them.
8. Enjoy.

4-INGREDIENT
Chicken Kabob Wraps

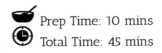 Prep Time: 10 mins

Total Time: 45 mins

Servings per Recipe: 1	
Calories	293.8
Fat	18.6g
Cholesterol	62.0mg
Sodium	406.4mg
Carbohydrates	14.4g
Protein	16.6g

Ingredients
1 1/2 lbs. boneless skinless chicken breasts
1 (1 lb.) package sliced turkey bacon
3/4 C. firmly packed brown sugar
2 tbsp chili powder

Directions
1. Before you do anything, preheat the oven to 350 F.
2. Slice the chicken breasts into 1-inch dices. Slice each bacon slice into 3 pieces.
3. Place a chicken cube on a bacon slice and roll it around it then thread it onto a skewer.
4. Repeat the process with the remaining chicken and bacon.
5. Get a mixing bowl: Combine in it the chili powder with brown sugar. Sprinkle it all over the chicken skewers.
6. Place the chicken skewers on a lined up baking pan. Cook them in the oven for 32 to 34 min.
7. Serve your chicken skewers warm.
8. Enjoy.

Cayenne Chicken Wraps with Cilantro Sauce

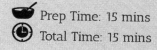 Prep Time: 15 mins

Total Time: 15 mins

Servings per Recipe: 4
Calories   278.7
Fat   16.3g
Cholesterol   87.5mg
Sodium   99.4mg
Carbohydrates   7.2g
Protein   25.3g

Ingredients

1 lb. boneless chicken breast
olive oil
1/2 tsp ground paprika
2 garlic cloves, minced
1 1/2 tsp fresh ginger, grated
salt
pepper
1 pinch cayenne
1 bell pepper, any color, seeded and sliced in strips

1 onion, sliced
1 tomatoes, seeded and diced
4 flatbread
Sauce
1/2 C. sour cream
1/8 C. chopped cilantro
1 green onion, chopped
2 tsp lime juice
salt
pepper

Directions

1. To prepare the sauce:
2. Get a mixing bowl: Whisk in it the sour cream with cilantro, onion, lime juice, a pinch of salt and pepper.
3. Place it in the fridge until ready to serve.
4. To prepare the wraps:
5. Flatten the chicken breasts until they become thin.
6. Get a mixing bowl: Stir in it the ginger, paprika and garlic powder together, salt, pepper, and cayenne.
7. Coat the chicken breasts with olive oil. Coat them with the spice mixture.
8. Before you do anything else, preheat the grill and grease it.
9. Cook in it the chicken breasts for 5 to 7 min on each side. Cut them into strips.
10. Place a large skillet over medium heat. Heat in it a swirl of olive oil.
11. Cook in it the onions with bell pepper, chicken strips and a pinch of salt for 4 min.
12. Divide the mixture between the tortillas then drizzle over them the cilantro sauce.
13. Fold your wraps tightly then serve them.
14. Enjoy.

ITALIAN
Guacamole Wraps

Prep Time: 10 mins
Total Time: 20 mins

Servings per Recipe: 2	
Calories	192.7
Fat	14.1g
Cholesterol	0.0mg
Sodium	34.5mg
Carbohydrates	16.2g
Protein	3.9g

Ingredients
2 zucchini, green and yellow julienned
1 onion, diced
1 red bell pepper, julienned
2 tbsp olive oil
1 C. Baby Spinach
1/2 C. guacamole

salt and pepper
flour tortilla
cherry tomatoes
Italian dressing

Directions
1. Place a skillet over medium heat. Heat in it the oil.
2. Cook in it the onion with bell pepper, zucchini, a pinch of salt and pepper for 11 min.
3. Place a tortilla on a serving plate. Spoon into it 2 tbsp of guacamole.
4. Top it with the stir fried veggies followed by spinach, tomato, and remaining guacamole.
5. Roll your tortilla tightly then serve it.
6. Enjoy.

Sweet Steak Rolls with Sesame Sauce

Prep Time: 20 mins
Total Time: 35 mins

Servings per Recipe: 1
Calories   394.2
Fat   11.3g
Cholesterol   64.2mg
Sodium   1504.2mg
Carbohydrates   44.9g
Protein   28.0g

Ingredients

Steak
1/2 tsp fresh ground black pepper
2 tsp salt
1 tbsp paprika
1/2 tsp cumin
1 tbsp brown sugar
1/4 tsp cayenne pepper
1 tsp allspice
2 tsp grated fresh ginger
1 tbsp chopped parsley
1 1/4 lbs. flank steaks

Sauce
1 tbsp light sesame oil
1 1/2 tbsp rice wine vinegar
2 tbsp light soy sauce
1 tbsp sugar
1 tbsp freshly grated ginger
1/2 jalapeno, grated

Slaw
3 scallions, sliced
8 C. Napa cabbage, sliced
1 carrot, shredded
1 C. cilantro, coarsely chopped
6 - 8 pita bread, wraps warm

Directions

1. To prepare the steak:
2. Get a zip lock bag. Place in it all the steak ingredients. Seal the bag and let them sit for an overnight.
3. Before you do anything else, preheat the grill and grease it.
4. Drain the steak and grill it for 9 to 12 min on each side. Place it aside to rest for 5 min then cut it into strips.
5. To prepare the sauce:
6. Get a mixing bowl: Whisk in it all the sauce ingredients.
7. Place a pan over medium heat. Cook in it the sauce for 2 min. Stir in the carrot with cabbage for 5 min.
8. Turn off the heat and stir in the cilantro.
9. Arrange the steak over the pita bread, top it with the cabbage and carrot mixture.
10. Roll your wraps burrito style. Serve them warm with extra toppings of your choice.
11. Enjoy.

EASY
Lunch Caesar Wraps

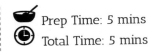 Prep Time: 5 mins

Total Time: 5 mins

Servings per Recipe: 2
Calories	25.5
Fat	1.5g
Cholesterol	4.4mg
Sodium	78.3mg
Carbohydrates	0.9g
Protein	2.2g

Ingredients
flour tortilla
1 C. shredded romaine lettuce
creamy caesar salad dressing
cooked chicken breast, chopped
2 tbsp grated parmesan cheese

Directions
1. Get a mixing bowl: Combine in it the lettuce with salad dressing, chicken breast, cheese, a pinch of salt and pepper.
2. Place the tortilla on a serving plate. Spoon the chicken mixture into the middle of it and wrap it.
3. Slice your tortilla in half then serve it.
4. Enjoy.

Tuscan Turkey Wraps

Prep Time: 2 mins
Total Time: 5 mins

Servings per Recipe: 1
Calories	256.4
Fat	5.9g
Cholesterol	38.6mg
Sodium	1445.5mg
Carbohydrates	33.0g
Protein	18.1g

Ingredients
1 whole wheat tortilla
1 (3/4 oz.) light swiss cheese
2 oz. deli turkey
1 Roma tomato, slices

3 - 4 basil leaves, torn
ground pepper

Directions
1. Place a pan over medium heat. Grease it with a cooking spray.
2. Place in it the tortilla and lay over it the cheese.
3. Top it with turkey, tomato, basil, a pinch of salt and pepper.
4. Fold the tortilla in half then serve it warm.
5. Enjoy.

KOREAN
Chicken Cutlet Wraps

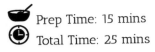 Prep Time: 15 mins

Total Time: 25 mins

Servings per Recipe: 4

Calories	300.8
Fat	10.5g
Cholesterol	72.6mg
Sodium	702.3mg
Carbohydrates	24.5g
Protein	26.9g

Ingredients

1 lb. chicken tenders, sliced
2 tbsp vegetable oil
2 tbsp fresh ginger, minced
4 garlic cloves, minced
1 red bell pepper, seeded and sliced thin
1 C. shredded cabbage and carrot coleslaw mix
3 green onions, sliced at an angle
1/2 C. plum sauce

2 C. basil leaves
1 tbsp fish sauce
1/2 head iceberg lettuce, halved again
1/2 seedless cucumber, chopped

Directions

1. Place a large pan over high heat. Heat in it the oil.
2. Cook in it the chicken tenders for 2 to 3 min on each side.
3. Stir in the ginger, garlic, bell pepper, cabbage and carrot mix and green onions.
4. Cook them for 2 to 3 min. Stir in the plum sauce and cook them for 2 min.
5. Fold the basil into the mixture with fish sauce. Turn off the heat.
6. Divide the mixture between lettuce leaves and place them on a serving plate.
7. Top them with cucumber then serve them right away.
8. Enjoy.

Chicken
Teriyaki Wraps

Prep Time: 5 mins
Total Time: 45 mins

Servings per Recipe: 2
Calories	633.8
Fat	32.1g
Cholesterol	195.0mg
Sodium	2912.9mg
Carbohydrates	42.0g
Protein	45.4g

Ingredients
1/4 C. water
1 tbsp cornstarch
1/2 C. teriyaki sauce
1 lb. ground chicken
1 (8 oz.) can water chestnuts, chopped

2 tbsp vegetable oil
rice noodles
shredded carrot
iceberg lettuce leaves

Directions
1. Get a small mixing bowl: mix in it the water with cornstarch until no lumps are found.
2. Add the teriyaki sauce and mix them well. Stir in the chicken with chestnuts. Refrigerate it for 40 min.
3. Place a large pan over medium heat. Heat in it the oil.
4. Drop in it mounds of the mixture and cook them for 2 to 3 min on each side.
5. Place the chicken fritters in lettuce leaves then serve them.
6. Enjoy.

ASIAN
Fusion Wraps

Prep Time: 20 mins
Total Time: 25 mins

Servings per Recipe: 6
Calories	188.3
Fat	11.4g
Cholesterol	25.4mg
Sodium	555.5mg
Carbohydrates	11.4g
Protein	11.3g

Ingredients
1 head iceberg lettuce
3 tbsp hoisin sauce
2 tbsp rice vinegar
1 tbsp water
2 boneless skinless chicken breasts, cut into strips
1 tsp kosher salt
2 tbsp canola oil
1 tbsp fresh ginger, peeled and chopped

1 medium carrot, julienned
2 green onions, chopped
1/2 C. roasted salted cashews

Directions
1. Get a mixing bowl: Whisk in it the hoisin, vinegar, and water. Place it aside.
2. Sprinkle some salt and pepper all over the chicken breasts.
3. Place a large skillet over medium heat. Heat in it the oil.
4. Cook in it the ginger for 12 sec. Stir in the chicken and cook them for 2 min.
5. Stir in the carrot and cook them for an extra 2 to 3 min. Stir in the vinegar mixture with green onion.
6. Cook them for 1 min. Turn off the heat and stir in the cashews.
7. Divide the chicken mixture between lettuce leaves. Serve your wraps immediately.
8. Enjoy.

Teriyaki Thursday Beef Wraps

🍳 Prep Time: 15 mins
🕐 Total Time: 17 mins

Servings per Recipe: 3
Calories	741.1
Fat	43.9 g
Cholesterol	138.3mg
Sodium	1306.7mg
Carbohydrates	30.1g
Protein	54.9 g

Ingredients

- 4 C. coleslaw mix
- 3 tbsp chopped parsley
- 2 tbsp rice vinegar
- 2 tbsp vegetable oil
- 2 tbsp light sesame oil
- 3/4 tsp ginger
- 1 1/2 lbs. lean boneless top round steaks, cut into strips
- 1/4 C. teriyaki sauce
- 4 -6 flour tortillas, round

Directions

1. Get a mixing bowl: Stir in it the steaks with teriyaki sauce. Cover it with a plastic and place it in the fridge for overnight.
2. Get a mixing bowl: Combine in the coleslaw mix with parsley, vinegar, sesame oil, a pinch of salt and pepper.
3. Place a large pan over high heat. Heat in it the oil. Stir fry in it the steak and teriyaki mix for 4 to 6 min.
4. Divide the steak mixture between the tortillas followed by the coleslaw salad.
5. Wrap your tortillas then serve them.
6. Enjoy.

HOUSTON
Club Wrap

Prep Time: 5 mins
Total Time: 5 mins

Servings per Recipe: 1
Calories	8.0
Fat	0.0g
Cholesterol	0.0mg
Sodium	5.8mg
Carbohydrates	1.6g
Protein	0.4g

Ingredients
1 leaf red leaf lettuce
1 slice turkey breast
1 slice chicken breast, optional
1 slice tomatoes
1 slice avocado, mashed
1 tsp lime juice
1 leaf arugula
1 tbsp sugar-free ranch dressing

Directions
1. Get a mixing bowl: Mix in it the avocado with lime juice and a pinch of salt to make the salsa.
2. Lay a lettuce leaf on a cutting board. Top it with turkey, chicken, tomato, avocado salsa, and arugula.
3. Wrap it around the filling tightly and press into it a toothpick to secure it.
4. Serve you wrap right away.
5. Enjoy.

Monroe
Chicken Wraps

Prep Time: 15 mins
Total Time: 15 mins

Servings per Recipe: 8
Calories	141.0
Fat	5.1g
Cholesterol	36.5mg
Sodium	43.9mg
Carbohydrates	9.4g
Protein	13.9g

Ingredients

1/4 C. raspberry preserves
2 tbsp olive oil
1 tbsp white wine vinegar
1 tsp Dijon mustard
salt & ground pepper
2 tbsp minced scallions

1 C. fresh raspberry
4 cooked chicken breast halves, cut into pieces
4 C. chopped Bibb lettuce

Directions

1. Get a mixing bowl: Mix in it the preserves, oil, vinegar, Dijon mustard and salt and pepper.
2. Stir in the scallions with raspberries and chicken.
3. Arrange the chopped lettuce on a serving plate. Spoon the chicken mixture over it.
4. Serve your loose chicken wrap right now.
5. Enjoy.

VENTURA
Wraps

Prep Time: 30 mins
Total Time: 30 mins

Servings per Recipe: 4
Calories   693.8
Fat   49.1g
Cholesterol   75.0mg
Sodium   886.0mg
Carbohydrates   54.3g
Protein   14.4g

Ingredients

1 (8 oz.) packages cream cheese, softened
1/2 C. sour cream
1 (4 oz.) cans chopped green chilies, drained
1 tbsp taco seasoning
4 (10 inches) flour tortillas, warmed

2 medium ripe avocados, peeled and sliced
2 plum tomatoes, sliced
5 green onions, sliced
1 (4 oz.) cans sliced ripe olives, drained

Directions

1. Get a mixing bowl: Whisk in it the cream cheese, sour cream, chilies and taco seasoning until they become smooth.

2. Place the tortillas on a serving plate. Pour 1/4 C. of cream over each tortilla.

3. Arrange over them the avocado with tomato, onion, and olives. Fold your tortillas then serve them.

4. Enjoy.

Black
Jack Wraps

Prep Time: 30 mins
Total Time: 40 mins

Servings per Recipe: 4	
Calories	528.2
Fat	20.3g
Cholesterol	25.1mg
Sodium	640.6mg
Carbohydrates	66.4g
Protein	21.9g

Ingredients

1 1/2 tbsp olive oil
2 cloves garlic, minced
1 C. chopped red bell pepper
1 C. chopped yellow bell pepper
1 C. chopped zucchini
1 C. chopped peeled yellow squash
1 C. chopped red onion
1 tsp ground cumin
1 tbsp chili powder

1/2 tsp oregano
salt and pepper
1 (15 oz.) cans black beans, drained
1 C. shredded Monterey jack pepper cheese
4 10-inch flour tortillas
4 tbsp chopped cilantro

Directions

1. Before you do anything, preheat the oven to 350 F.
2. Place a large skillet over medium heat. Heat in it the oil.
3. Cook in it the garlic, peppers, zucchini, squash, and onion for 10 min.
4. Stir in the cumin, chili powder, oregano, and salt and pepper. Cook them for 1 min.
5. Get a mixing bowl: Mash in it the beans until they become chunky.
6. Fold into it the cooked veggies with cheese.
7. Spread 1/4 of the bean mixture over each tortilla. Top them with 1 tbsp of cilantro then wrap them.
8. Place them with the seam facing down on a baking pan.
9. Lay a piece of foil on top to cover them. Cook them in the oven for 12 min.
10. Slice you wraps in half then serve them warm.
11. Enjoy.

TUESDAY'S
Tuna Wraps

Prep Time: 10 mins
Total Time: 10 mins

Servings per Recipe: 6
Calories	191.1
Fat	9.8g
Cholesterol	34.2mg
Sodium	393.2mg
Carbohydrates	10.2g
Protein	15.5g

Ingredients
2 (6 oz.) cans tuna in water
1/2 C. mayonnaise
4 tbsp celery, chopped
4 tbsp white onions, chopped
3 tbsp red apples, chopped
1/4 C. dried sweetened cranberries
1/4 C. Colby-Monterey Jack cheese,
shredded
1/4 tsp minced garlic
salt and pepper
6 9-inch spinach tortillas

Directions
1. Get a mixing bowl: Stir in it the tuna with mayo, celery, onion, apples, cranberries, cheese, garlic, a pinch of salt and pepper.
2. Divide the mixture between the tortillas then wrap them tightly. Serve them immediately.
3. Enjoy.

Chipotle Corn Wraps

Prep Time: 15 mins
Total Time: 15 mins

Servings per Recipe: 2
Calories   433.3
Fat   28.7g
Cholesterol   61.8mg
Sodium   346.0mg
Carbohydrates   26.3g
Protein   20.9g

Ingredients

2 (12 inches) whole wheat tortillas, any flavor
1 1/2 tbsp cream cheese
1 tsp chipotle chile in adobo
4 leaves lettuce
4 slices Monterey jack pepper cheese
4 slices tomatoes

1/2 avocado, sliced
4 slices red onions
1/2 C. jicama, sliced into matchsticks
1/4 C. sweet corn, defrosted
1/2 C. cooked black beans, drained and rinsed

Directions

1. Place the tortillas on baking sheet. Top them with cream cheese, lettuce, jack cheese, tomato, avocado, onion, and jicama.
2. Top them with corn, bean, a pinch of salt and pepper. Wrap your tortillas tightly then serve them.
3. Enjoy.

SHRIMP WRAPS
with Lemon Mayo

Prep Time: 20 mins
Total Time: 30 mins

Servings per Recipe: 8
Calories   300.0
Fat   15.6g
Cholesterol   115.8mg
Sodium   593.3mg
Carbohydrates   19.1g
Protein   20.0g

Ingredients

1 lb. shrimp, cooked and diced
4 (8 inches) flour tortillas, warmed
6 oz. brie cheese, ripe and diced
2 2/3 C. mixed greens
1/2 C. tomatoes, seeds removed and diced
4 slices crisp cooked turkey bacon,
crumbled
Lemon Mayo
1/2 C. mayonnaise
1 tbsp lemon juice
1 tsp fresh dill

Directions

1. Get a small mixing bowl: Whisk in it the mayo with dill and lemon juice to make the sauce.
2. Place a skillet over medium heat. Coat it with a cooking spray.
3. Cook in it the brie cheese with shrimp, a pinch of salt and pepper for 2 min.
4. Place the tortillas on a baking sheet. Spoon into the shrimp mixture followed by mixed greens, tomato, and bacon.
5. Fold your tortillas then serve them warm.
6. Enjoy.

Oregon
Turkey Wraps

Prep Time: 20 mins
Total Time: 20 mins

Servings per Recipe: 1
Calories	35.6
Fat	1.6g
Cholesterol	3.4mg
Sodium	58.0mg
Carbohydrates	4.6g
Protein	0.8g

Ingredients

6 tortillas
8 oz. cream cheese
6 -12 tbsp pepper jelly
6 leaves romaine lettuce
24 slices turkey breast

12 slices roasted bell peppers
12 slices sun-dried tomatoes
1/4 C. sliced black olives

Directions

1. Place the tortillas on a baking sheet. Top them with cream cheese, jelly, lettuce, turkey, sundried tomatoes, and olives.
2. Wrap your tortillas tightly burrito style. Serve them immediately.
3. Enjoy.

HONEY MUSTARD
Chicken Wraps

🥣 Prep Time: 20 mins
🕐 Total Time: 50 mins

Servings per Recipe: 4
Calories	460.7
Fat	10.9g
Cholesterol	48.9mg
Sodium	781.3mg
Carbohydrates	66.3g
Protein	32.0g

Ingredients

2 boneless skinless chicken breasts
1 tbsp olive oil
2 tbsp garlic salt
2 tbsp parsley
2 tbsp basil
1 tsp chicken bouillon
6 (3/4 oz.) wedges Laughing Cow light swiss cheese
1 - 2 tbsp cilantro leaf, chopped

1/3 C. honey
1/3 C. Dijon mustard
4 flour tortillas
4 romaine leaves
1 cucumber, peeled and sliced lengthwise into strips
1 small red onion, sliced
1 tomatoes, sliced

Directions

1. Before you do anything, preheat the oven to 350 F.
2. Coat a baking sheet with a cooking spray. Place it aside.
3. Coat the chicken breasts with olive oil.
4. Get a small mixing bowl: Mix in it the garlic salt, parsley, basil and chicken bouillon.
5. Massage the mixture into the chicken breasts. Place them on the greased sheet and bake them for 40 min.
6. Place them aside to rest for 5 min then cut them into strips.
7. Get a mixing bowl: Whisk in it the honey with mustard.
8. Lay the tortillas on a baking pan.
9. Top them with the cilantro cheese mix followed 1 tbsp of honey and mustard sauce, romaine leaf, and chicken strips.
10. Add cucumber with onion and tomato. Fold your tortillas tightly then serve them with extra toppings of your choice.
11. Enjoy.

Baja Wraps

🍳 Prep Time: 15 mins
🕐 Total Time: 25 mins

Servings per Recipe: 4
Calories   233.8
Fat   1.2g
Cholesterol   0.0mg
Sodium   6.8mg
Carbohydrates   50.9g
Protein   9.1g

Ingredients

1 red bell pepper, seeded, chopped
1 green bell pepper, seeded, chopped
1 onion, peeled, sliced
1 (15 oz.) cans black beans, low sodium, drained, rinsed

2 mangoes, peeled, pitted, chopped
1 lime, juice
1/2 C. fresh cilantro, chopped
1 avocado, peeled, pitted, diced
4 (10 inches) fat-free tortillas

Directions

1. Place a large skillet over medium heat. Coat it with a cooking spray.
2. Cook in it the bell peppers with onion for 6 min. Stir in the beans and cook them for extra 6 min.
3. Get a mixing bowl: Stir in it the mangoes, lime juice, and cilantro to make the salsa.
4. Spoon the bell pepper and beans mixture into the tortillas. Top them with the mango salsa and roll them tightly.
5. Slice your wraps in half then serve them.
6. Enjoy.

ORGANIC
Chicken Wraps

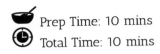 Prep Time: 10 mins
Total Time: 10 mins

Servings per Recipe: 2

Calories	116.6
Fat	3.2g
Cholesterol	36.5mg
Sodium	94.6mg
Carbohydrates	6.7g
Protein	15.7g

Ingredients
2 tbsp hummus, see appendix
4 small organic whole wheat tortillas
1 large grilled or pan fried chicken breast,
cut into strips
1/2 small cucumber, cut into strips

4 medium romaine lettuce leaves, shredded
4 tsp chili oil
kosher sea salt
ground pepper

Directions
1. Place the tortillas on a cutting board. Coat each one of them with 1/2 tbsp of hummus.
2. Top them with chicken strips, cucumber, lettuce, 1 tsp of chili oil, a pinch of salt and pepper.
3. Wrap the tortillas then serve them.
4. Enjoy.

Classical
Cobb Wraps

Prep Time: 15 mins
Total Time: 15 mins

Servings per Recipe: 4
Calories   428.9
Fat   31.8g
Cholesterol   51.4mg
Sodium   874.2mg
Carbohydrates   21.5g
Protein   14.3g

Ingredients

1 boneless skinless chicken breast, cooked and chopped
12 slices turkey bacon
4 flour tortillas, burrito size
4 C. mixed salad greens
1 1/3 C. grape tomatoes, halved
1 C. cucumber, sliced

1/4 C. red onion, thinly sliced
4 tbsp blue cheese, crumbled
1/2 C. ranch dressing
2 hard-boiled eggs, chopped
avocado, sliced

Directions

1. Place a large pan over medium heat. Fry in it the bacon until it becomes crunchy. Drain it and chop it.
2. Warm the tortillas for few seconds in the microwave.
3. Place them on serving plates. Top them with salad greens, tomatoes, cucumbers, onion, eggs, chicken, dressing and blue cheese.
4. Roll your tortillas tightly then serve them.
5. Enjoy.

HOW TO MAKE
a Hummus Wrap

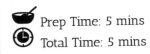

Prep Time: 5 mins
Total Time: 5 mins

Servings per Recipe: 2
Calories   149.5
Fat   5.3g
Cholesterol   0.0mg
Sodium   311.4mg
Carbohydrates   20.8g
Protein   5.2g

Ingredients
2 flour tortillas
1/4 C. hummus, see appendix
1/4 C. chopped tomato
1/4 C. spinach, shredded
olive oil
1 tsp minced sweet onion

Directions
1. Place the tortillas on a cutting board. Coat one side of them with the hummus.
2. Arrange over them the tomato slices followed by spinach, onion, some olive oil, and a pinch of salt.
3. Wrap your tortilla tightly then serve it.
4. Enjoy.

Country
Vegetable Wraps

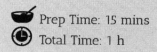 Prep Time: 15 mins
⏱ Total Time: 1 h

Servings per Recipe: 6
Calories	250.2
Fat	21.6g
Cholesterol	2.2mg
Sodium	65.0mg
Carbohydrates	12.3g
Protein	4.8g

Ingredients
Veggies
1 eggplant, peeled cubed
1 zucchini, cubed
1 yellow squash, cubed
8 oz. mushrooms, quartered
1 red onion, sliced
1 red bell pepper, cut into strips
3 garlic cloves, sliced
1/2 C. olive oil
salt and pepper
Spread
4 C. raw spinach

3 garlic cloves
1/3 C. low-fat mayonnaise
1 tbsp vegetable oil
3 tbsp parmesan cheese
salt and pepper
Wrap
6 burrito-size low-fat flour tortillas

Directions
1. Before you do anything, preheat the grill and grease it.
2. Get a large roasting pan. Toss in it the veggies with oil, salt, and pepper.
3. Place the garlic in a small piece of foil and wrap it around it.
4. Lay it along with the other veggies on the grill. Cook them for 12 to 16 min until they become soft.
5. Get a blender: Place in it all the spinach spread ingredients. Blend them smooth.
6. Spread the mixture over the tortillas. Top them with the grilled veggies and wrap them tightly.
7. Serve your wraps warm.
8. Enjoy.

ANGELA'S
Beef Wraps

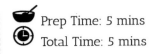 Prep Time: 5 mins

Total Time: 5 mins

Servings per Recipe: 1

Calories	677.5
Fat	26.9g
Cholesterol	113.5mg
Sodium	942.2mg
Carbohydrates	60.8g
Protein	47.2g

Ingredients
1 large flour tortilla
chive & onion cream cheese
ranch dressing
prepared horseradish
3 - 5 leaves romaine lettuce, torn
2 slices tomatoes, cut into strips

1/4 C. shredded Monterey jack pepper cheese
4 - 5 slices of Angus roast beef

Directions
1. Place a tortilla on a serving plate. Lay over it some onion and cream cheese followed by beef roast.
2. Drizzle over it some ranch dressing. Top them with some horseradish sauce followed by lettuce, tomato, and cheese.
3. Sprinkle over them a pinch of salt and pepper. Wrap it in a burrito style. Serve it right away.
4. Enjoy.

Picnic
Chicken Wraps

Prep Time: 10 mins
Total Time: 20 mins

Servings per Recipe: 4	
Calories	530.7
Fat	19.5g
Cholesterol	24.9mg
Sodium	988.9mg
Carbohydrates	69.1g
Protein	20.2g

Ingredients

2 tbsp olive oil
1 onion, chopped
2 garlic cloves, crushed
1 (16 oz.) packages broccoli coleslaw mix
1 C. shredded cabbage
3/4 C. cooked chicken breast, cut into pieces
1 dash pepper
1 dash salt
1 (15 oz.) cans garbanzo beans, undrained
3 tbsp mayonnaise
2 tbsp Dijon mustard

1 tsp ground cumin
4 garlic cloves, minced
1 tsp onion powder
1 tsp lemon pepper
salt
pepper
4 (10 inches) flour tortillas

Directions

1. Place a pan over high heat. Heat in it the oil. Cook in it the onion with 2 cloves of garlic for 4 min.
2. Add the coleslaw mix and let them cook for 2 min. Stir in the chicken with cabbage, a pinch of salt and pepper.
3. Cook them for 1 min. Turn off the heat and place it aside.
4. Get a food processor: Place in it the garbanzo beans, mayonnaise, mustard, cumin, remaining garlic, onion powder, lemon powder, salt, and pepper.
5. Process them until they become smooth.
6. Warm up the tortillas for few seconds in the microwave. Spread on side of them the beans mixture.
7. Arrange over them the cabbage mixture then fold them burrito style.
8. Serve your wraps right away with extra toppings if you desire.
9. Enjoy.

BAKED
Fish Wraps

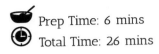
Prep Time: 6 mins
Total Time: 26 mins

Servings per Recipe: 4
Calories   491.6
Fat   24.3g
Cholesterol   39.1mg
Sodium   1326.4mg
Carbohydrates   52.0g
Protein   16.0g

Ingredients

1 small onion, diced
14.5 cream of mushroom soup
1 tbsp sweet chili sauce
14.5 oz. light sour cream
1/2 C. light cheese, grated
6 flour tortillas
12 frozen fish sticks
1/4 C. extra light cheese, grated

Directions

1. Before you do anything, preheat the oven to 365 F.
2. Get a mixing bowl: Stir in it the onion, soup, sweet chili sauce, sour cream and 1/2 C. grated cheese to make the sauce.
3. Arrange 2 fish fingers on a tortilla. Drizzle over it 2 tbsp of cream sauce.
4. Fold it and place it in a greased baking dish.
5. Repeat the process with the remaining tortillas. Pour the remaining cream sauce on top.
6. Sprinkle the rest of the cheese over them. Place the dish in the oven and let it cook for 16 to 22 min.
7. Enjoy.

American
Sloppy Joe Wraps

Prep Time: 30 mins
Total Time: 1 hr 10 mins

Servings per Recipe: 6
Calories	429.0
Fat	15.9g
Cholesterol	49.1mg
Sodium	933.4mg
Carbohydrates	49.0g
Protein	23.1g

Ingredients
1 tbsp vegetable oil
1 stalk celery, diced
1 large onion, chopped
2 cloves garlic, minced
2 tbsp chili powder
1 tbsp brown sugar

1/2 tsp salt
1 lb. lean ground beef
1 (28 oz.) cans canned tomatoes, with puree
6 10-inch flour tortillas, warmed
1/2 head iceberg lettuce, shredded

Directions
1. Place a large pan over medium heat. Heat in it the oil.
2. Cook in it the onion with celery for 14 min.
3. Add the garlic with chili powder, brown sugar, and salt. Let them cook for 3 min.
4. Stir in the beef and cook them for 15 min until it is done.
5. Stir in the tomato. Let them cook for an extra 12 min until the mixture becomes thick.
6. Spoon 3/4 of the beef mixture into each tortilla.
7. Arrange over it the shredded lettuce then wrap them burrito style. Serve them right away.
8. Enjoy.

CHICAGO
Inspired Roast Beef Wraps

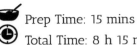

Prep Time: 15 mins
Total Time: 8 h 15 mins

Servings per Recipe: 8
Calories	597.6
Fat	29.5g
Cholesterol	82.9mg
Sodium	1255.3mg
Carbohydrates	51.8g
Protein	31.2g

Ingredients
1/2 C. sour cream
1/2 C. mayonnaise
1 green onion, chopped
2 tbsp prepared horseradish
1/2 tsp salt
1/2 tsp pepper
8 (12 inches) flour tortillas

1 lb. roast beef, cut into slices
2 (6 oz.) packages deli-style sharp cheddar cheese slices
2 C. shredded iceberg lettuce
1 tomatoes, sliced

Directions
1. Get a mixing bowl: Mix in it the sour cream with mayo, onion, horseradish, salt, and pepper.
2. Divide the mixture between the tortillas. Top them with roasted beef slices, lettuce, tomato, and cheese.
3. Fold the tortillas over the filling then wrap them with a cling wrap.
4. Place the wraps in the fridge for an overnight then serve them.
5. Enjoy.

Hot
Tofu Wraps

Prep Time: 5 mins
Total Time: 15 mins

Servings per Recipe: 1
Calories	368.8
Fat	30.2g
Cholesterol	39.5mg
Sodium	533.3mg
Carbohydrates	9.0g
Protein	18.9g

Ingredients
1 whole wheat sandwich wrap
1/2 C. tomatoes, slices
1 C. chopped lettuce
1/2 C. extra firm tofu, diced
2 tbsp ranch dressing

1/4 C. shredded cheddar cheese
2 tbsp buffalo, sauce
2 tbsp hot sauce

Directions
1. Place a skillet over medium heat. Heat in it a splash of oil.
2. Cook in it the tofu dices until they become golden. Drain them and place them aside.
3. Place the wrap on a serving plate.
4. Top it with ranch dressing, followed by lettuce, tomato, tofu, buffalo sauce, hot sauce, and cheese.
5. Fold the sandwich burrito style then serve it.
6. Enjoy.

CAJUN
Black Yam Wraps

Prep Time: 10 mins
Total Time: 20 mins

Servings per Recipe: 6
Calories   508.6
Fat   14.6g
Cholesterol   0.0mg
Sodium   556.4mg
Carbohydrates   81.4g
Protein   14.6g

Ingredients

2 yams, shredded
1 (15 oz.) cans black beans, drained, rinsed
1 C. red onion, chopped
4 green onions, sliced
1/2 C. sunflower seeds, shelled

1/4 C. Italian dressing
2 tsp honey
6 (10 inches) flour tortillas, warmed to soften

Directions

1. Place a pan over medium heat. Grease it with a cooking spray.
2. Cook in it the yams for 6 min. Drain them and place them aside.
3. Coat the same pan with a cooking spray. Cook in t the onion for 6 min.
4. Stir in the cooked yams with beans, green onion, sunflower seeds, a pinch of salt and pepper.
5. Get a mixing bowl: Combine in it the honey with dressing, beans mixture, a pinch of salt and pepper.
6. Spoon the mixture into tortillas then wrap them burrito style. Serve them immediately.
7. Enjoy.

New York Cheddar Turkey Wrap

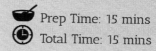

Prep Time: 15 mins
Total Time: 15 mins

Servings per Recipe: 3
Calories	257.7
Fat	15.5g
Cholesterol	62.5mg
Sodium	759.3mg
Carbohydrates	14.8g
Protein	15.6g

Ingredients
- 3 tbsp plain nonfat yogurt
- 1 tbsp reduced-fat mayonnaise
- 1 -2 tsp Dijon mustard
- 1 large tart apple, cored and sliced into 16 wedges
- 4 oz. cheddar cheese, cut into 16 slices
- 4 oz. deli turkey, slice into 16 strips

Directions
1. Get a mixing bowl: Whisk in it the yogurt, mayo, and mustard to make the dressing.
2. Place an apple wedge on a plate next to a cheese slice. Wrap around them a turkey slice.
3. Repeat the process with the remaining ingredients to make more wraps.
4. Serve them with the dressing.
5. Enjoy.

HANDMADE
Flax Wraps

Prep Time: 5 mins
Total Time: 13 mins

Servings per Recipe: 1
Calories   357.9
Fat   31.4g
Cholesterol   186.0mg
Sodium   290.3mg
Carbohydrates   10.3g
Protein   12.0g

Ingredients

3 tbsp ground flax seeds
1/4 tsp baking powder
1/4 tsp onion powder
1/4 tsp paprika
1 pinch sea salt

1 tbsp coconut oil, melted
1 tbsp water
1 egg
coconut oil

Directions

1. Get a mixing bowl: Mix in it the flax seeds with baking powder, onion powder, paprika, and salt.
2. Get a mixing bowl: Whisk in it the water with eggs until they become frothy.
3. Add to them the dry ingredients with coconut oil. Mix them until no lumps are found.
4. Coat a microwave-safe plate with some coconut oil. Pour in it the batter in an even layer.
5. Place it in the microwave and cook it for 3 min on high. Place the bread wrap aside to rest for 6 min.
6. Serve your bread wrap with your desired filling.
7. Enjoy.

Picnic
Hummus Wraps

Prep Time: 5 mins
Total Time: 5 mins

Servings per Recipe: 2
Calories	194.2
Fat	11.2g
Cholesterol	13.4mg
Sodium	537.0mg
Carbohydrates	18.1g
Protein	8.6g

Ingredients
1 soft cracker bread, halved, or pita
4 oz. hummus, see appendix
1/4 C. parsley, chopped
8 ripe olives, sliced

1 small cucumber, sliced
1 small tomatoes, seeded and chopped
1-oz feta cheese, crumbled

Directions
1. Place the bread on a serving plate. Top it with hummus, parsley, cucumber, olives, tomato, and cheese.
2. Wrap the bread around the filling then serve it.
3. Enjoy.

CHILI
Crunch Wraps

Prep Time: 5 mins
Total Time: 10 mins

Servings per Recipe: 4
Calories   488.2
Fat   22.2g
Cholesterol   52.7mg
Sodium   1329.4mg
Carbohydrates   53.4g
Protein   20.7g

Ingredients
1 (19 oz.) cans mild plain chili, heated
3 C. Fritos corn chips
1 C. mild cheddar cheese, shredded

1/4-1/2 C. onion, diced
4 large burrito-size flour tortillas

Directions
1. Get a mixing bowl: Stir in it the Fritos with chili. Spoon the mixture into the tortillas.
2. Rope them with cheese and onion. Fold the tortillas over the filling burrito style.
3. Microwave the wraps for 20 seconds on high then serve them warm.
4. Enjoy.

2nd Street
Beef Wraps

Prep Time: 30 mins
Total Time: 30 mins

Servings per Recipe: 6
Calories	213.3
Fat	7.7g
Cholesterol	28.7mg
Sodium	835.1mg
Carbohydrates	22.9g
Protein	12.8g

Ingredients
3 oz. blue cheese, crumbled
2 tbsp horseradish
2 tbsp low-fat mayonnaise
1/2 tsp black pepper
2 tbsp rice wine vinegar
1 tbsp honey
1 garlic clove, minced
2 C. cabbage, sliced

1/4 C. celery, sliced
1/4 C. onion, sliced
1/4 C. red bell pepper, sliced
1/2 lb. deli roast beef, sliced
6 flour tortillas

Directions
1. Get a mixing bowl: Stir in it the blue cheese, horseradish, mayonnaise, and 1/4 tsp pepper to make the dressing.
2. Get a large mixing bowl: Whisk in it 1 tbsp of the dressing with vinegar, honey, and garlic.
3. Stir in the cabbage, celery, onion, and bell pepper. Season them with a pinch of salt and pepper.
4. Place the tortilla on a baking sheet. Place in it the tortillas and top them with the cheese dressing.
5. Divide the veggies mixture between tortillas then top them with beef slices.
6. Wrap the tortillas over the filling burrito-style then serve them.
7. Enjoy.

GREEK
Meatball Wraps

Prep Time: 20 mins
Total Time: 30 mins

Servings per Recipe: 6
Calories   232.8
Fat   7.9g
Cholesterol   67.1mg
Sodium   191.6mg
Carbohydrates   18.4g
Protein   22.3g

Ingredients

Meatballs
1 1/4 lbs. lean ground turkey
1/4 C. chopped onion
1 1/2 tsp dried oregano
1/2 tsp dried mint
1/2 tsp parsley
1/2 tsp lemon pepper
1 garlic clove, minced
1 tsp lemon juice

Sauce
1/2 C. nonfat sour cream
1/2 medium cucumber, peeled and chopped
1 1/2 tsp lemon juice
1/8 tsp black pepper
Other
3 (6 inches) pita bread, halved crosswise
6 lettuce leaves, torn into pieces
1 medium tomatoes, chopped

Directions

1. Get a large mixing bowl: Mix in it all the meatballs ingredients. Shape the mixture into bite-size meatballs.

2. Place a pan over medium heat. Coat it with a cooking spray. Brown in it the meatballs for 9 min or longer until fully done.

3. Get a mixing bowl: Stir in it all the cucumber salsa ingredients.

4. Divide the meatballs between the pita bread. Top them with tomato, lettuce and cucumber salsa.

5. Either stuff your pita, or top them and fold.

6. Enjoy.

Olive
Turkey Wraps

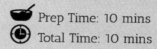
Prep Time: 10 mins
Total Time: 10 mins

Servings per Recipe: 1
Calories	42.4
Fat	1.5g
Cholesterol	4.7mg
Sodium	138.9mg
Carbohydrates	5.0g
Protein	2.0g

Ingredients
1/2 C. kraft cream cheese with chives and onions
1/2 C. feta cheese, crumbled
1/4 black olives, chopped
32 inches flour tortilla
4 oz. smoked turkey, sliced

1 C. loosely packed thoroughly washed spinach leaves
1/4-1/2 tsp oregano

Directions
1. Get a mixing bowl: Mix in it the cream cheese, feta cheese, olives, and oregano.
2. Spoon the mixture into the tortilla in an even layer. Top it turkey and spinach.
3. Fold the tortilla over the filling then wrap it in a cling foil. Place it in the fridge for 70 min.
4. Once the time is up, slice your wrap into 3 pieces then serve them.
5. Enjoy.

CHEDDAR
Salsa Wraps

Prep Time: 10 mins
Total Time: 15 mins

Servings per Recipe: 4
Calories   467.0
Fat   22.1g
Cholesterol   77.8mg
Sodium   722.4mg
Carbohydrates   40.4g
Protein   25.6g

Ingredients

2 avocados, pitted peeled and sliced
2 (16 oz.) cans black beans, drained and rinsed
2 large tomatoes, diced
4 oz. salsa
1/2 tsp cumin

1/4 C. cilantro
1/4 C. cheddar cheese, shredded
4 oz. spinach
4 tortillas

Directions

1. Get a mixing bowl: Stir in it the avocado, beans, tomato, salsa, cumin, and cilantro.

2. Spoon the mixture into the tortillas. Arrange over them the spinach and cheese.

3. Fold your tortillas burrito style then serve them.

4. Enjoy.

Redmond
Veggie Wraps

🥣 Prep Time: 15 mins
🕐 Total Time: 23 mins

Servings per Recipe: 1
Calories	335.5
Fat	11.8g
Cholesterol	0.3mg
Sodium	89.8mg
Carbohydrates	50.5g
Protein	16.4g

Ingredients
24 asparagus spears
1 ripe avocado, pitted and peeled
1 tbsp lime juice
1 garlic clove, minced
1 1/2 C. cooked long-grain brown rice, cold

3 tbsp plain nonfat yogurt
3 (10 inches) whole wheat tortillas
1/3 C. cilantro leaf
2 tbsp chopped red onions

Directions
1. Place a large saucepan over high heat. Heat in it 2 inches of water.
2. Place over it a basket and cook in it the asparagus with a lid on for 7 to 9 min.
3. Once the time is up, place it in an ice bowl and drain it.
4. Get a mixing bowl: Mix in it the avocado, lime juice, and garlic to make the salsa.
5. Get a mixing bowl: Mix in it the rice with yogurt.
6. Place a large skillet over medium heat. Warm in it the tortillas for few seconds on each side.
7. Place the tortillas on serving plates. Top them with the avocado salsa followed by the yogurt mixture, asparagus, cilantro, and onion.
8. Fold your tortillas burrito style. Wrap them in a cling foil and place them in the fridge for 70 min.
9. Once the time is up, slice your wraps in half then serve them.
10. Enjoy.

SESAME
Crab Wraps

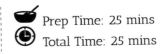

Prep Time: 25 mins
Total Time: 25 mins

Servings per Recipe: 1
Calories	15.6
Fat	0.9g
Cholesterol	0.0mg
Sodium	5.1mg
Carbohydrates	1.6g
Protein	0.4g

Ingredients
15 rice paper sheets
1/2 C. green cabbage, chopped
1/2 C. fresh carrot, chopped
1/2 C. sweet onion, chopped
1/4 C. celery, chopped

1/4 C. sweet green pepper, chopped
3 tbsp black sesame seeds
5 oz. imitation crabmeat
oriental sweet chili sauce

Directions
1. Get a mixing bowl: Stir in it the cabbage with carrot, onion, celery, green pepper, sesame seeds, crab meat, a pinch of salt and pepper.
2. Place a rice sheet in some warm water and let it sit for 1 min. Drain it and place it on a kitchen towel.
3. Place on one side of it 2 tbsp of the crab mixture. Drizzle over it 1 tsp of chili sauce.
4. Pull the sides of the sheet over the filling then roll it forward over the filling.
5. Place it on a serving plate then repeat the process with the remaining ingredients.
6. Serve your crab wraps immediately.
7. Enjoy.

Pittsburgh
Deli Wraps

Prep Time: 5 mins
Total Time: 15 mins

Servings per Recipe: 4
Calories   229.7
Fat   11.8g
Cholesterol   29.7mg
Sodium   432.3mg
Carbohydrates   22.2g
Protein   8.8g

Ingredients
4 slices turkey bacon
4 flour tortillas
3 oz. gouda cheese, sliced

4 oz. roasted turkey deli meat, sliced
1 medium apple, sliced
baby greens

Directions
1. Place a large skillet over medium heat. Cook in it the bacon until it becomes crisp. Drain it and place it aside.
2. Place the tortillas on a plate. Top them with cheese, turkey, apple slices, bacon and baby greens.
3. Fold the tortilla wraps then serve them.
4. Enjoy.

ROASTED
Chicken Wraps with Cucumber Relish

Prep Time: 20 mins
Total Time: 35 mins

Servings per Recipe: 4	
Calories	528.6
Fat	20.4g
Cholesterol	81.4mg
Sodium	1223.9mg
Carbohydrates	53.2g
Protein	33.6g

Ingredients
Wraps
4 pita bread
4 tbsp yogurt
Marinade
1/2 C. yogurt
2 tbsp honey
2 tsp lemon juice
2 tsp lemon zest
2 tsp hot sauce
1 large garlic clove, minced
1 tsp dried oregano
1/2 tsp ground cumin
1/4 tsp ground pepper
1/2 tsp salt

4 boneless skinless chicken breasts
Relish
1 English cucumber, halved lengthwise and sliced
1/2 tsp salt
1 C. diced tomato, diced
1/2 C. diced red onion, diced
6 tbsp black olives, chopped and pitted
4 tbsp fresh parsley, chopped
2 tbsp fresh dill weed, chopped
1 garlic clove, minced
4 tbsp extra virgin olive oil
4 tsp fresh lemon juice

Directions
1. To prepare the chicken:
2. Get a mixing bowl: Mix in it all the marinade ingredients. Pour it into a large zip lock bag.
3. Add to it the chicken breasts and seal it. Place it in the fridge to sit for 3 h.
4. Place the cucumber slices in a bowl. Season them with some salt and let them sit for 35 min.
5. Drain them and transfer them to a large mixing bowl.
6. Add to them the tomato, onion, olives, parsley, dill, garlic, olive oil and lemon juice.
7. Place the relish in the fridge for 1 h 30 min.
8. Before you do anything, preheat the grill and grease it.
9. Drain the chicken breasts and cook them for 6 to 8 min on each side.
10. Allow them to rest for 4 min then slice them into strips.
11. Arrange the chicken slices in pita bread.
12. Top them with the cucumber relish then serve them with some sour cream.
13. Enjoy.

Monterey Mexicorn Wraps

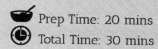

Prep Time: 20 mins
Total Time: 30 mins

Servings per Recipe: 4

Calories	220.5
Fat	5.4g
Cholesterol	13.4mg
Sodium	449.5mg
Carbohydrates	33.5g
Protein	12.5g

Ingredients

1 (15 oz.) cans black beans, drained and rinsed
1 (11 oz.) cans mexicorn, drained
2 oz. shredded Monterey jack cheese
1/4 C. chopped cilantro
1/4 C. bottled salsa
4 (8 - 9 inch) jalapeno-cilantro tortillas

Directions

1. Before you do anything, preheat the oven to 350 F.
2. Get a mixing bowl: Stir in it the black beans, corn, cheese, cilantro, and salsa.
3. Divide the mixture between the tortillas. Roll them tightly then wrap them in foil.
4. Place them on a baking tray and cook them for 11 min in the oven.
5. Serve your wraps with some extra guacamole and salsa.
6. Enjoy.

TSO'S
Shrimp Wraps

Prep Time: 10 mins
Total Time: 15 mins

Servings per Recipe: 4
Calories   169.0
Fat   1.6g
Cholesterol   43.5mg
Sodium   573.7mg
Carbohydrates   32.8g
Protein   6.9g

Ingredients
16 large shrimp, peeled and deveined
vegetable oil
1 tsp crushed red pepper flakes
salt and pepper

1/3 C. orange marmalade
1/2 C. hoisin sauce
bibb lettuce
1/4 cucumber, julienne slice

Directions
1. Before you do anything, preheat the grill and grease it.
2. Get a mixing bowl: Stir in it the shrimp with some oil, crushed pepper, salt, and pepper.
3. Thread the shrimp onto wooden skewers. Place them on the grill and cook them for 2 to 3 min on each side.
4. Get a mixing bowl: Mix in it the orange marmalade with hoisin sauce.
5. Arrange the shrimp on lettuce leaves. Drizzle over them some marmalade sauce then top them with cucumber.
6. Serve your wraps immediately.
7. Enjoy.

Sonoma
Country Wraps

Prep Time: 5 mins
Total Time: 5 mins

Servings per Recipe: 1
Calories   579.2
Fat   27.1g
Cholesterol   64.0mg
Sodium   1012.8mg
Carbohydrates   54.9g
Protein   28.0g

Ingredients

1 (12 inches) flour tortillas
1/3 C. red seedless California grapes, halved
2 oz. grilled chicken breasts, sliced
1 tbsp creamy caesar salad dressing

1 C. romaine lettuce, chopped
1 tbsp parmesan cheese, shredded
caesar crouton

Directions

1. Get a mixing bowl: Mix in it the grapes with chicken caesar salad dressing, lettuce, and cheese.
2. Warm the tortilla for few seconds in the microwave.
3. Place it on a plate. Spoon in it the chicken mixture and wrap it tightly.
4. Serve your wrap right away.
5. Enjoy.

BROWN RICE
Arizona Wraps

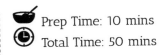

Prep Time: 10 mins
Total Time: 50 mins

Servings per Recipe: 1
Calories	355.1
Fat	12.6g
Cholesterol	29.6mg
Sodium	625.1mg
Carbohydrates	45.3g
Protein	15.4g

Ingredients
1 C. brown rice, uncooked
2 C. water
12 oz. Pace Picante Sauce
2 C. cheddar cheese, shredded

15 oz. black beans, drained and rinsed
8 -10 flour tortillas, burrito size

Directions
1. Prepare the rice by following the instructions on the package. Fluff it with a fork.
2. Get a large mixing bowl: Stir in it the rice with beans, Picante sauce, a pinch of salt and pepper.
3. Divide the mixture between the tortillas. Top them with cheese then fold them burrito style.
4. Heat your wraps in the microwave for few seconds then serve them with a sauce of your choice.
5. Enjoy.

Weeknight
Burrito Wraps

Prep Time: 20 mins
Total Time: 30 mins

Servings per Recipe: 4
Calories   440.5
Fat   15.3g
Cholesterol   53.0mg
Sodium   927.3mg
Carbohydrates   49.0g
Protein   26.0g

Ingredients

1/2 lb. extra lean ground beef
1 C. canned black beans, drained and rinsed
1/3 C. chunky salsa
2 tbsp sliced green onions
1/2 C. shredded Monterey jack cheese

1/2 C. shredded lettuce
1/2 C. chopped tomato
4 tbsp sour cream
4 burrito-size flour tortillas

Directions

1. Place a large pan over medium heat. Brown in it the beef for 6 min. Discard the excess fat.
2. Stir in the beans and cook them for 4 min. Spoon the mixture into the tortillas.
3. Top them with chunky salsa, green onions, cheese, lettuce, tomato and sour cream.
4. Wrap your tortillas over the filling burrito style.
5. Wrap your burritos in a piece of foil then heat them for few seconds in the microwave.
6. Serve your burritos warm with extra toppings of your choice.
7. Enjoy.

PB&J
Wraps

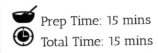
Prep Time: 15 mins

Total Time: 15 mins

Servings per Recipe: 4
Calories   420.1
Fat   30.8g
Cholesterol   62.4mg
Sodium   523.4mg
Carbohydrates   27.0g
Protein   10.9g

Ingredients

1 (8 oz.) packages cream cheese
1/4 C. peanut butter
4 (6 inches) flour tortillas
6 tbsp fruit spread

Directions

1. Get a mixing bowl: Mix in it the cream cheese until it becomes smooth and soft.

2. Mix in the peanut butter. Spoon the mixture into the tortillas and spread them in an even layer.

3. Top them with the fruit spread then roll them tightly.

4. Slice your fruity wraps in half then serve them.

5. Enjoy.

Mesa
Mediterranean Chicken Wraps

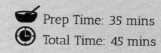 Prep Time: 35 mins

Total Time: 45 mins

Servings per Recipe: 2
Calories	1169.8
Fat	51.3g
Cholesterol	169.4mg
Sodium	1654.5mg
Carbohydrates	108.5g
Protein	69.1g

Ingredients

4 boneless skinless chicken breasts
2 garlic cloves, crushed
1/4 tsp ground cinnamon
1 tsp ground allspice
1/2 tsp black pepper
1 tbsp olive oil
3 tbsp lemon juice
2 tbsp plain yogurt

Wraps

4 pita bread
shredded lettuce
2 - 3 tomatoes, sliced
6 - 8 radishes, sliced

Spicy Mayo

1 C. mayonnaise
1 green chile, seeded and chopped
1 tbsp chopped coriander
1 tbsp lime juice

Directions

1. Slice the breasts into 3 slices.
2. Get a large mixing bowl: Mix in it the garlic, cinnamon, allspice, pepper, oil, lemon juice, and yogurt.
3. Stir in the chicken slices to coat them with the mixture. Put on the lid and place it in the fridge for 1 h.
4. Before you do anything else, preheat the grill and grease it.
5. Press the chicken strips onto skewers. Grill them for 4 to 6 min on each side until they are done.
6. Get a mixing bowl: Whisk in it the mayo with chile, coriander, and lime juice.
7. Open the pita bread. Arrange in them the grilled chicken followed by lettuce, tomato, radishes, and chili mayo.
8. Season them with some salt and pepper. Serve your chicken wraps immediately.
9. Enjoy.

MEXICANA
Wraps

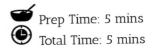 Prep Time: 5 mins

Total Time: 5 mins

Servings per Recipe: 1

Calories	254.5
Fat	6.5g
Cholesterol	7.4mg
Sodium	749.2mg
Carbohydrates	36.8g
Protein	11.2g

Ingredients
1 tortilla, wrap
1 (3/4 oz.) wedge swiss cheese
2 thick roasted red peppers

Directions
1. Place a small pan over medium heat. Heat in it the bell pepper for 1 min.
2. Place a tortilla on a serving plate. Spread over it the swiss cheese.
3. Arrange the roasted pepper slices on top. Roll the tortilla over it tightly then serve it.
4. Enjoy.

Trinidad
Rotisserie Wraps

Prep Time: 15 mins
Total Time: 15 mins

Servings per Recipe: 2
Calories   157.7
Fat   12.9g
Cholesterol   0.0mg
Sodium   5.1mg
Carbohydrates   11.0g
Protein   2.3g

Ingredients

1 1/2 C. rotisserie chicken, cold and chopped
1/2 C. fresh mango, diced
1/4 C. green onion, sliced
1/4 C. red bell pepper, diced

1/4 C. macadamia nuts, chopped
1/4 C. salad dressing
6 - 8 butter lettuce leaves

Directions

1. Get a mixing bowl: Toss in it the chicken with mango, green onion, bell pepper, macadamia nuts, and cilantro dressing.
2. Divide the mixture between the lettuce leaves then serve them.
3. Enjoy.

GARDEN
Turkey Pesto Wraps

Prep Time: 5 mins
Total Time: 5 mins

Servings per Recipe: 1
Calories   461.0
Fat   14.1g
Cholesterol   14.8mg
Sodium   835.2mg
Carbohydrates   69.0g
Protein   16.4g

Ingredients
1 large tortilla
2 tbsp basil pesto
3 tbsp fat-free cream cheese
3 slices tomatoes
6 slices cucumbers

1/4 C. alfalfa sprout
2 tbsp shredded cheddar cheese
2 tbsp shredded carrots
4 slices deli turkey

Directions
1. Warm the tortilla in a pan for few seconds on each side. Transfer it to a plate.
2. Top it with pesto sauce, followed by cream cheese, tomato, cucumbers, alfalfa sprouts, carrot, turkey, and cheese.
3. Roll your tortilla burrito style then serve it.
4. Enjoy.

Picante
Bean Wraps

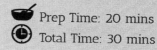 Prep Time: 20 mins

Total Time: 30 mins

Servings per Recipe: 2

Calories	871.9
Fat	19.9g
Cholesterol	37.7mg
Sodium	875.6mg
Carbohydrates	136.2g
Protein	36.5g

Ingredients

1 (15 1/2 oz.) cans black beans, drained
1/2 C. chopped red bell pepper
1/2 C. chopped yellow bell pepper
3/4 C. cooked long-grain white rice, warm
1/4 C. chopped cilantro

1/4 C. Picante sauce
1 tbsp hot adobo sauce
1/2 tsp ground cumin
3/4 C. shredded Monterey jack cheese
2 10-inch flour tortillas

Directions

1. Place a large saucepan over medium heat. Stir in it the beans for 4 min.
2. Stir in the bell peppers with rice, cilantro, Picante sauce, adobo sauce, cumin, a pinch of salt and pepper.
3. Spoon the mixture into the tortillas and spread them in an even layer.
4. Sprinkle the cheese on top then rolls them tightly. Slice your bean rolls in half then serve them.
5. Enjoy.

MEDITERRANEAN
Cheese Wraps

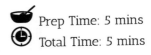

Prep Time: 5 mins
Total Time: 5 mins

Servings per Recipe: 1

Calories	333.1
Fat	20.2g
Cholesterol	124.3mg
Sodium	2207.9mg
Carbohydrates	2.4g
Protein	33.4g

Ingredients

1 whole wheat sandwich wrap
2 oz. deli roast beef
1-oz chevre cheese

1 tsp light mayonnaise
lettuce
tomatoes

Directions

1. Heat the tortilla in the microwave for few seconds. Transfer it to a serving plate.

2. Top it with a layer of mayo, lettuce, tomato, roast beef, and goat cheese.

3. Roll your tortilla over the filling tightly then serve it.

4. Enjoy.

Japanese
Spring Roll Wraps

Prep Time: 20 mins
Total Time: 25 mins

Servings per Recipe: 1
Calories   187.8
Fat   9.1g
Cholesterol   23.0mg
Sodium   2054.0mg
Carbohydrates   4.9g
Protein   22.0g

Ingredients

4 rice paper sheets
25 g vermicelli rice noodles
100 g smoked salmon
1 tsp extra virgin olive oil
1 tbsp capers
2 medium mushrooms, diced

1/2 C. cabbage, diced
1 tbsp soy sauce
1 tbsp sweet chili sauce
1/4 tsp ground black pepper

Directions

1. Prepare the noodles by following the instructions on the package. Drain it.
2. Get a large mixing bowl: Mix in it the noodles with the rest of the ingredients except for the rice paper sheets.
3. Place the filling in the fridge for 12 min.
4. Place a rice sheet in some warm water for 2 min. Drain it and place it on a kitchen towel.
5. Spoon 1/4 of the filling on one side of it. Pull the sides of the sheet over the filling then roll it tightly.
6. Repeat the process with the remaining ingredients.
7. Serve your vermicelli Rolls immediately with your favorite dipping sauce.
8. Enjoy.

DIJON
Turkey Wraps

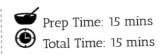

Prep Time: 15 mins
Total Time: 15 mins

Servings per Recipe: 1
Calories   1104.3
Fat   63.6g
Cholesterol   47.2mg
Sodium   7971.9mg
Carbohydrates   101.4g
Protein   44.8g

Ingredients

1 tbsp cider vinegar
salt
pepper
1/2 medium red onion, sliced
2 small firm avocados, cut in wedges
4 large flour tortillas
4 oz. baby spring greens

6 oz. turkey, sliced and cut into strips
Spread
3 tbsp Dijon mustard
2 tbsp balsamic vinegar
1/4 C. mayonnaise

Directions

1. Get a mixing bowl: Whisk in it the mustard with vinegar, and mayo.

2. Spread the mixture all over the tortillas leaving the sides empty.

3. Top them with a layer of onion, avocados, turkey and spring onions.

4. Season them with some salt. Roll the tortilla over the filling tightly then serve them.

5. Enjoy.

Pesto Tilapia Lettuce Wraps

Prep Time: 20 mins
Total Time: 40 mins

Servings per Recipe: 2
Calories   3041.5
Fat   284.2g
Cholesterol   177.5mg
Sodium   2460.3mg
Carbohydrates   84.1g
Protein   54.8g

Ingredients

2 - 3 tilapia fillets
1 avocado, sliced
16 oz. canola oil
1 head iceberg lettuce

Batter

1 tsp Old Bay Seasoning
1 tsp salt
1 tsp black pepper
1 tsp cayenne pepper
1/2 tsp garlic powder
3/4 C. wheat flour
3/4 C. panko breadcrumbs

1 egg
1/2-1 C. water

Pesto

1/2 C. roasted red pepper
1/4 C. Greek yogurt
2 garlic cloves
1/2 C. bunch basil
1/2 C. parmesan and pecorino cheese blend
1/2 tsp pepper
1/4 C. olive oil

Directions

1. To prepare the batter:
2. Get a mixing bowl:: Mix in it the all the batter ingredients.
3. Cut each fish fillet into 3 pieces. Dip them completely in the batter.
4. Place a large deep pan over medium heat. Heat in it 3 inches of oil.
5. Deep fry in it the fish pieces until they become golden brown. Drain them and place them on paper towels to dry.
6. Get a food processor: Place in it all the pepper pesto ingredients. Season them with a pinch of salt. Blend them smooth.
7. Overlap each 2 lettuce leaves on a serving plate. Top them with fried fish followed by avocado and pepper pesto.
8. Serve your open wraps immediately.
9. Enjoy.

BANGKOK
Meets Morocco Wraps

Prep Time: 5 mins
Total Time: 15 mins

Servings per Recipe: 6
Calories   202.0
Fat   4.0g
Cholesterol   0.1mg
Sodium   615.5mg
Carbohydrates   34.9g
Protein   7.3g

Ingredients
2 (14 oz.) cans chickpeas, drained and rinsed
1 tbsp Thai style chili sauce or sriracha
2 tbsp hoisin sauce
1 tbsp low sodium soy sauce
1 tbsp olive oil
2 tbsp rice vinegar

1/2 tbsp sugar
1 tsp red pepper flakes
1 tbsp hot sauce
1/2 C. chopped basil
6 - 8 lettuce leaves, Bibb

Directions
1. Get a blender: Place in it the chickpeas and pulse them several times until they become chunky.
2. Place a large skillet over medium heat. Heat in it 1 tbsp of olive oil.
3. Cook in it the chunky chickpeas for 4 min while stirring all the time.
4. Stir in the chili and hoisin sauce with soy sauce, rice vinegar, sugar, red pepper flakes, hot sauce, a pinch of salt and pepper.
5. Lower the heat and let them cook for 12 min. Stir in the basil leaves and cook them for 1 min.
6. Spoon the chickpea mixture into the lettuce wraps. Serve them right away.
7. Enjoy.

American
Bacon Lettuce and Tomato Wraps

Prep Time: 12 mins
Total Time: 12 mins

Servings per Recipe: 4	
Calories	451.4
Fat	22.2g
Cholesterol	41.5mg
Sodium	1133.9mg
Carbohydrates	39.9g
Protein	22.3g

Ingredients

3 C. romaine lettuce leaves, torn
1 medium tomatoes, chopped
1/3 C. turkey bacon, crisply cooked, crumbled

1/4 C. caesar salad dressing
1 1/2 C. Sargento artisan blends shredded parmesan cheese
4 (10 inches) flour tortillas

Directions

1. Get a mixing bowl: Stir in it the lettuce, tomato, bacon, salad dressing, and cheese.
2. Divide the mixture between the tortillas. Wrap them in the shape of burritos.
3. Serve your sandwiches immediately or refrigerate them until ready to serve.
4. Enjoy.

CASHEW
Butter Wraps

Prep Time: 5 mins
Total Time: 5 mins

Servings per Recipe: 2
Calories	133.5
Fat	0.8g
Cholesterol	0.0mg
Sodium	14.6mg
Carbohydrates	32.4g
Protein	3.3g

Ingredients
8 tbsp raw smooth cashew butter, divided
into 2 tsp per leaf
12 romaine lettuce leaves
2 bananas, sliced

Directions
1. Lay 2 tsp of cashew butter in each lettuce leaf.
2. Arrange over it the banana slices then serve them right away.
3. Enjoy.

Guyanese Chickpea Wraps

Prep Time: 10 mins
Total Time: 1 h 20 mins

Servings per Recipe: 8
Calories	200.6
Fat	6.7g
Cholesterol	0.0mg
Sodium	612.4mg
Carbohydrates	30.2g
Protein	6.2g

Ingredients

3 tbsp vegetable oil
2 C. onions, diced
5 garlic cloves, minced
1/2 chili pepper, seeded and diced
fresh ginger, peeled and minced
3 tbsp curry powder
1 tsp ground cumin
1/4 tsp cayenne
1/4 tsp ground turmeric

1 tsp salt
2 (15 oz.) cans chickpeas, drained and rinsed
whole wheat tortilla
hot sauce
red onion, diced
cucumber, diced

Directions

1. Place a deep pan over medium heat. Heat in it the oil.
2. Cook in it the onion for 9 min. Stir in the garlic, chili pepper, and ginger. Cook them for 3 min.
3. Stir in the spices and cook them for 1 min. Stir in the chickpeas with 3 C. of water.
4. Cook them until they start simmering. Lower the heat and let them cook until the mixture becomes thick for about 1 h.
5. Heat the tortilla in the microwave for few seconds. Transfer it to a serving plate.
6. Spoon the chickpea mixture into the tortilla. Top it with some hot sauce, onion, and cucumber.
7. Fold the tortilla over the filling burrito-style then serve it.
8. Enjoy.

SPICY
Turkey Wraps

Prep Time: 20 mins
Total Time: 40 mins

Servings per Recipe: 8
Calories   80.0
Fat   1.7g
Cholesterol   26.6mg
Sodium   181.4mg
Carbohydrates   4.8g
Protein   10.6g

Ingredients
1 medium onion, chopped
1 medium sweet potato, peeled and cut into pieces
1 (14 oz.) cans low sodium reduced-fat chicken broth
3 tbsp diced celery
1/2 tsp salt
1 tsp sage

1/4 tsp black pepper
2 C. boneless cooked turkey, cubed
3/4 C. seasoned stuffing mix
8 (10 inches) whole wheat tortillas
2 C. shredded reduced-fat cheddar cheese
sliced jalapeno pepper

Directions
1. Place a pot over medium heat. Stir in it the onion, sweet potato, chicken broth, celery, salt, sage, and pepper.
2. Cook them until they start simmering. Lower the heat and let them cook for 12 min.
3. Add the stuffing mix with turkey. Let them cook for 6 min while stirring until the mixture becomes thick.
4. Warm a tortilla in the microwave for few seconds. Place it on a serving plate.
5. Spread in the center of it 1/4 C. of cheese followed by 1/2 C. of the turkey mixture.
6. Fold the tortilla over the filling burrito style. Place it in a hot pan and cook it for few seconds on each side.
7. Repeat the process with the remaining cheese, turkey mixture and tortillas.
8. Serve your wraps warm.
9. Enjoy.

West African
Peanut Wraps

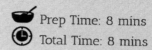 Prep Time: 8 mins

Total Time: 8 mins

Servings per Recipe: 2
Calories	49.6
Fat	2.3g
Cholesterol	0.0mg
Sodium	283.3mg
Carbohydrates	5.9g
Protein	2.4g

Ingredients

1 C. cooked shrimp
1 tomatoes, seeded and chopped
1/4 C. carrot, shredded
2 tbsp of mint, chopped
1 tsp lemon zest, grated

1 tbsp reduced sodium soy sauce
1 large fat-free flour tortillas
1 tbsp peanuts, chopped

Directions

1. Get a mixing bowl: Toss in it the shrimp, chopped tomato, shredded carrot, chopped mint, grated lemon zest, and soy sauce.
2. Season them with a pinch of salt.
3. Pour the mixture in the center of a tortilla. Fold it burrito style then serve it.
4. Enjoy.

MEXICAN
Tuna Rolls

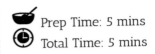

Prep Time: 5 mins
Total Time: 5 mins

Servings per Recipe: 1
Calories	294.6
Fat	7.5g
Cholesterol	32.3mg
Sodium	500.1mg
Carbohydrates	30.6g
Protein	25.7g

Ingredients
1 whole wheat tortilla
2 tbsp guacamole
0.5 (6 oz.) cans tuna, drained
2 medium romaine lettuce leaves
1 small tomatoes, sliced

Directions
1. Warm the tortilla in a hot pan for few seconds on each side.
2. Transfer it to a serving plate. Top it with a layer of guacamole, tuna, lettuce, and tomato.
3. Season them with a pinch of salt and pepper. Roll the tortilla over the filling tightly.
4. Slice your tuna roll in half then serve it.
5. Enjoy.

Moscow
Beef Wraps

Prep Time: 5 mins
Total Time: 9 mins

Servings per Recipe: 1
Calories	371.9
Fat	22.7g
Cholesterol	111.8mg
Sodium	156.0mg
Carbohydrates	4.0g
Protein	38.0g

Ingredients
1 large whole wheat tortilla
mayonnaise
3 -6 slices roast beef
1/8 C. sliced bell peppers

sliced tomatoes
2 slices swiss cheese
1/8 C. lettuce

Directions
1. Warm the tortilla in the microwave for few seconds.
2. Top it with a layer of a dressing followed by lettuce, tomato, pepper, onion, beef roast, and cheese.
3. Fold the tortilla over the filling burrito-style then serve it.
4. Enjoy.

CHIPOTLE
Bean Wraps

Prep Time: 25 mins
Total Time: 25 mins

Servings per Recipe: 4
Calories	399.8
Fat	14.3g
Cholesterol	0.0mg
Sodium	633.1mg
Carbohydrates	56.7g
Protein	13.8g

Ingredients
2 tbsp cider vinegar
1 tbsp canola oil
2 tsp chopped canned chipotle chilies in adobo
1/4 tsp salt
2 C. shredded red cabbage
1 medium carrot, shredded

1/4 C. chopped cilantro
1 (15 oz.) cans white beans, rinsed
1 ripe avocado
1/2 C. shredded sharp cheddar cheese
2 tbsp minced red onions
4 whole wheat tortillas

Directions
1. Get a mixing bowl: Mix in it the vinegar, oil, chipotle chile and salt.
2. Stir in the carrot with cabbage, and cilantro. place it aside.
3. Get a mixing bowl: Mix in it the avocado with beans until they become chunky.
4. Fold the cheese and onion into the mixture.
5. Warm the tortillas in the microwave for few seconds. Top them with a layer of avocado spread followed by cabbage salad.
6. Roll the tortillas over the filling tightly. Serve them immediately.
7. Enjoy.

Hot
Hawaiian Wraps

Prep Time: 10 mins
Total Time: 40 mins

Servings per Recipe: 6
Calories   558.5
Fat   38.0g
Cholesterol   56.9mg
Sodium   1119.5mg
Carbohydrates   44.0g
Protein   9.5g

Ingredients
1 (20 oz.) cans, pineapple chunks drained
1 lb. turkey bacon
1/2 C. Miracle Whip

1/2 C. chili sauce or sriracha
1 C. brown sugar

Directions
1. Before you do anything, preheat the oven to 400 F.
2. Slice the bacon strips in half.
3. Roll a bacon slice around each pineapple chunk then press into it a toothpick to secure it.
4. Repeat the process with the remaining bacon and pineapple. Lay them in a baking dish.
5. Cook them in the oven for 11 min.
6. Get a mixing bowl: Whisk in it the miracle whip with chili sauce and brown sugar.
7. Drizzle it all over the bacon wraps. Cook them for an extra 22 min in the oven.
8. Serve your chili wraps warm.
9. Enjoy.

NAPA
Valley Wraps

Prep Time: 15 mins
Total Time: 15 mins

Servings per Recipe: 4
Calories   416.7
Fat   9.5g
Cholesterol   0.0mg
Sodium   155.1mg
Carbohydrates   77.8g
Protein   25.0g

Ingredients
3 oranges peeled and sliced.
1/2 avocado
2 sprigs dill
1/2 head napa cabbage, sliced

2 tomatoes, sliced
12 romaine leaves

Directions
1. Get a food processor: Place in it 2 slices oranges with dill and avocado.
2. Blend them smooth to make the dressing.
3. Get a large mixing bowl: Chop the remaining orange and stir it with cabbage and orange dressing.
4. Spoon the mixture into romaine leaves. Garnish them with tomato slices then serve them.
5. Enjoy.

California
Wraps with Thai Spicy Mayo

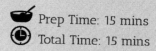

Prep Time: 15 mins
Total Time: 15 mins

Servings per Recipe: 2
Calories	550.4
Fat	30.0g
Cholesterol	60.2mg
Sodium	998.5mg
Carbohydrates	48.9g
Protein	21.5g

Ingredients

Sauce
3 tbsp mayonnaise
1 tbsp Thai sweet chili sauce or garlic sriracha
1 tsp Worcestershire sauce
1 tsp chili powder
1/8 tsp sriracha sauce
Filling
1/2 C. swiss cheese, shredded
1/2 C. cheddar cheese, shredded
1/4 C. spinach, chopped
1/4 C. portabella mushroom, chopped

2 tbsp red bell peppers, chopped
1/4 C. summer squash, grated
3 tbsp sweet onions, chopped
1 tbsp basil, chopped
salt
ground black pepper
2 (10 inches) tortillas
Toppings
chopped tomato
cubed avocado
chips, crushed
mixed sprouts

Directions

1. Get a large mixing bowl: Whisk in it the mayo with sweet chili sauce, Worcestershire sauce, chili powder and Sriracha sauce.
2. Stir in the cheese with spinach, mushrooms, bell pepper, squash, onion, and basil. Sprinkle over them some salt and pepper.
3. Spoon the mixture into the tortillas and fold them. Serve your wraps right away.
4. Enjoy.

KETOGENIC
String Bean Wraps

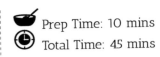 Prep Time: 10 mins

Total Time: 45 mins

Servings per Recipe: 6

Calories	117.2
Fat	7.5g
Cholesterol	10.8mg
Sodium	141.7mg
Carbohydrates	9.9g
Protein	4.4g

Ingredients
2 (15 oz.) cans green beans
12 slices turkey bacon

Directions
1. Before you do anything, preheat the oven to 375 F.
2. Gather 5 green beans in your hands. Wrap around them a bacon slice and place them on a baking sheet.
3. Repeat the process with the remaining ingredients. Season them with a pinch of salt and pepper.
4. Broil them in the oven for 36 min.
5. Enjoy.

Hot Breakfast Wraps

Prep Time: 5 mins
Total Time: 5 mins

Servings per Recipe: 1
Calories	1611.0
Fat	103.6g
Cholesterol	3362.2mg
Sodium	2071.5mg
Carbohydrates	41.0g
Protein	118.4g

Ingredients

1 whole wheat tortilla
1 tbsp reduced-fat mayonnaise
1 tbsp hot sauce
2 medium hard-boiled eggs, shelled and chopped
4 tbsp sweet onions, chopped
6 tbsp lettuce, chopped

Directions

1. Get a mixing bowl: Whisk in it the mayo with hot sauce.
2. Add the eggs with onion, lettuce, a pinch of salt and pepper. Toss them to coat.
3. Spoon the mixture into one side of the tortilla then roll it tightly.
4. Serve your wrap right away.
5. Enjoy.

SIMPLE
Pesto

Prep Time: 2 mins
Total Time: 12 mins

Servings per Recipe: 6
Calories   199 kcal
Fat   21.1 g
Carbohydrates   2g
Protein   1.7 g
Cholesterol   0 mg
Sodium   389 mg

Ingredients

1/4 C. almonds
3 cloves garlic
1 1/2 C. fresh basil leaves
1/2 C. olive oil
1 pinch ground nutmeg
salt and pepper to taste

Directions

1. Set your oven to 450 degrees F before doing anything else.
2. Arrange the almonds onto a cookie sheet and bake for about 10 minutes or till toasted slightly.
3. In a food processor, add the toasted almonds and the remaining ingredients till a rough paste forms.

How to Make
Hummus

🥣 Prep Time: 10 mins
🕐 Total Time: 10 mins

Servings per Recipe: 16
Calories	77 kcal
Fat	4.3 g
Carbohydrates	8.1g
Protein	2.6 g
Cholesterol	0 mg
Sodium	236 mg

Ingredients
2 C. canned garbanzo beans, drained
1/3 C. tahini
1/4 C. lemon juice
1 tsp salt
2 cloves garlic, halved

1 tbsp olive oil
1 pinch paprika
1 tsp minced fresh parsley

Directions
1. Blend the following in a food processer until paste-like: garlic, garbanzos, salt, tahini, and lemon juice.
2. Add this to a bowl with olive oil, paprika, and parsley.
3. Enjoy.

HOW TO MAKE
Japanese Style Teriyaki Sauce

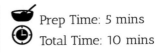

Prep Time: 5 mins
Total Time: 10 mins

Servings per Recipe: 4
Calories   57 kcal
Fat   0 g
Carbohydrates   7.4g
Protein   1.1 g
Cholesterol   0 mg
Sodium   902 mg

Ingredients

1/4 C. dark soy sauce
1/4 C. sake
2 tbsps mirin, optional
1 tbsp white sugar

Directions

1. Get a bowl mix: sugar, soy sauce, mirin, and sake.

2. Work everything by hand until it is completely smooth and uniform.

3. Place the sauce in the fridge until it is cold.

4. Enjoy.

Printed in Great Britain
by Amazon

60796073R00059